World of Design

Bowls and Boxes

Anne Civardi

Photography by Sam Hare & Jane Paszkiewicz

SEA-TO-SEA

Mankato Collingwood London

This edition first published in 2010 by
Sea-to-Sea Publications
Distributed by Black Rabbit Books
P.O. Box 3263
Mankato, Minnesota 56002

Copyright © Sea-to-Sea Publications 2010

Printed in USA

9 8 7 6 5 4 3 2

Published by arrangement with the Watts Publishing
Group Ltd., London.

Library of Congress Cataloging-in-Publication Data
Civardi, Anne.
  Bowls and boxes / Anne Civardi ; photography by
Sam Hare & Jane Paszkiewicz.
       p. cm. -- (World of design)
  Includes bibliographical references and index.
  ISBN 978-1-59771-210-1 (hardcover : alk. paper)
  1. Handicraft--Juvenile literature. 2. Containers--Juvenile
literature. I. Hare, Sam. II. Paszkiewicz, Jane. III. Title.
  TT157.C476 2010
  745.5--dc22
                                              2008043070

Design: Rachel Hamdi and Holly Fulbrook
Editor: Ruth Thomson
The author would like to thank Joss Graham
(www.jossgrahamgallery@btopenworld.com),
Ruth and Neil Thomson and Islington Education Library
Service (www.objectlessons.org) for the loan of items from
their collection.

Contents

South African recycled papier-mâché bowls

Kashmiri painted paper pulp trinket box

All kinds of containers

For thousands of years, craftspeople all over the world have designed and created containers in all sorts of shapes, sizes, colors, and materials.

Bowls, dishes, jugs, boxes, baskets, refuse bins, and bottles are all containers. They may be made from clay, wood, paper, dried grasses, and reeds, fruits, tree roots, seaweed, and even ostrich eggs.

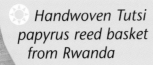

Handwoven Tutsi papyrus reed basket from Rwanda

Old Moroccan terra-cotta wine vessel

Woven cat-shaped bamboo basket from the Philippines

Painted wooden boxes from Poland

Painted and fired clay pitcher from Mexico

Carved calabash bowl from West Africa

Many containers are designed to hold or store things, such as water or milk, bread, grains, jewelry, or flowers. Others have been created simply for decoration. Some have handles for carrying, or spouts for pouring. Some have lids, others are open. They can be deep or shallow, big or small, round or square.

This book will help you understand how people design and create containers. It will also show you how to make your own bowls, boxes, and baskets using those from around the world as inspiration.

Ethiopian woven-grass breadbasket

Mexican painted gourd box

Horse-shaped, wooden inkwell from India

5

Clay creations

All these pots and dishes are made of clay and then baked in a hot oven, called a kiln, to make them hard and strong.

This brightly colored round French pot was designed with a spout, handle, and lid for serving tea.

Look closer

- The cats' faces have been designed to fit the shape of the pot exactly.
- The whiskers almost touch each other.
- Their pointed ears curl under the rim.
- The noses are extra long.

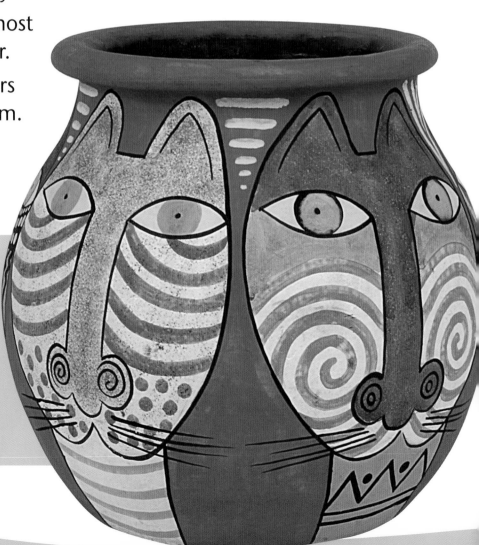

This South African pot was formed from sausage-shaped coils of clay, laid on top of each other. The potter smoothed the surface to hold the coils together and then painted on the cats' faces before the pot was fired (baked hard).

Look closer

- The bright colors on this fishy bowl were created by mixing liquid clay with dyes.
- Some fish are solid, while others are simple outlines.
- The fish look like they are swimming around the bowl, following one another.

☼ *To make this Moroccan bowl waterproof, it was coated in a liquid, called glaze. Then it was fired in a kiln to make it hard and glossy.*

Look closer

- The geometric design on this pot was pressed or scratched on while the clay was still wet.

☼ *Long ago, this old Indian pot was filled with liquid opium, which was used with a quill pen to sign important documents.*

Look closer

- The terra-cotta pot on the right was designed to look like a bird with wings and a beak.
- It has legs to stand on.

☼ *Mexican coil pots, like this, were often found in graves with offerings for the dead to take into the next world. It is more than 500 years old.*

A clay coil pot

1 Roll a small lump of clay into a ball. Roll the ball into a fat sausage shape. Keep rolling until you have a long, even, thin sausage shape.

You will need

- self-hardening clay
- a board to roll on
- a paintbrush
- poster or acrylic paints

wooden board

2 Coil the sausage shape around and around to make the base of the pot.

3 Roll more sausage shapes. Lay them in coils, one on top of the other, on the base. Each one should be long enough to make a layer of the pot.

Join the ends together (see page 31).

4 Shape your pot as you go. Make sure each coil is firmly stuck to the one below. When the pot is finished, leave it in a warm place to dry.

Tip: Instead of keeping the coils, you could smooth the outside of the pot and paint on animal faces, like the cat pot on page 6.

5 Paint each coil a different color.

9

Paper pulp containers

Paper pulp is cheap and strong. It can be easily molded into beautiful bowls, boxes, and dishes.

The size and shape of this Indian pulp box was made to hold a ball of string.

Look closer

- The pattern on the lid of the string box above joins perfectly with that of the base.

- It fills the surface without any of the details overlapping.

- The flowers and leaves have been delicately painted in pastel colors that blend together.

This brightly colored box from Kashmir has been varnished to keep the paint from getting damaged and to make the box strong and glossy.

- Compare the bold patterns and bright colors of this paper holder and bowl with those of the string box opposite.

Although this bowl and box from Bihar in India have not been varnished, they are still very strong. Paper pulp is so tough that it can be used to make tables and chairs.

Look closer

- The paper pulp lids of these boxes have been molded into the shape of the chicken's head and tail and the tortoise's shell.

- The artist has used gold paint to make the boxes look luxurious.

Craftspeople in Kashmir create trinket boxes, like this chicken and tortoise. Boxes like these were first made from pulp left over from papermaking.

11

A pulpy paper holder

- paper pulp (see page 30)
- a small box ● plastic wrap
- poster paints and a paintbrush
- notepaper ● scissors
- thin ribbon

1 First make some paper pulp (see page 30). Then cover a small box with plastic wrap, making sure it covers the rim.

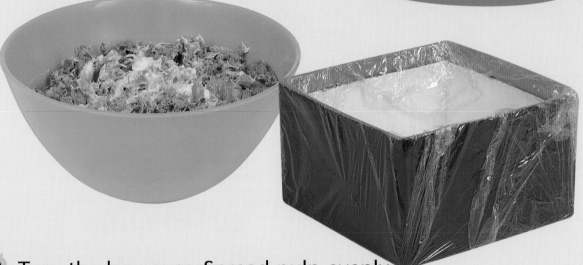

2 Turn the box over. Spread pulp evenly over the bottom and sides. Make sure the pulp is at least ½in (1cm) thick. Leave it to dry in a warm place.

Tip: The pulp will take about two days to dry.

12

3 Carefully separate the pulp box from the small box and peel off the plastic wrap. Paint the box a bright color.

4 When the paint is dry, paint a bold, colorful pattern on the box.

5 To make an ideal gift, fill the box with colored notepaper, tied with a ribbon.

Containers from nature

All over the world, people make useful containers from things they find in nature.

☼ In a tiny village high up in the Andes mountains, in South America, whole families carve gourds, like this, with pictures of everyday scenes, myths, and celebrations.

This gourd is the hollow, dried shell of a South American fruit. It has been finely carved with a tool called a *buril*.

Look closer

- The carving shows farmers plowing a field with their oxen.
- The dark colors were made by pressing burning pieces of wood into the gourd's surface.

☼ This ostrich egg was used as a water container by a nomad who roamed the desert in Yemen. He filled it at waterholes through a hole drilled in the top of the thick shell and sealed it tight with a leather plug.

14

- This big gourd container is decorated with cowrie shells and beaded figures and animals to show a hunting scene.

- There is a man holding a bow and arrow and a beaded ostrich.

✷ *Made in Mali, West Africa, this gourd was probably used to carry water or to store grain.*

- The calabash bowl below is carved, trimmed with leather, and decorated with cowrie shells hanging on leather strips.

✷ *Brightly colored faces have been painted on this coconut shell container from the Far East.*

✷ *West African women make bowls, like this, from half a calabash fruit, to carry milk or water, or as a musical instrument.*

A pumpkin lantern

Tip: Choose a big, round pumpkin. Pumpkins are fruits similar to gourds and are easy to carve.

You will need

- a big pumpkin ● a fine felt-tip pen
- a knife ● a big metal spoon
- a fat candle

You will need an adult to help you carve this pumpkin.

1 Draw a spiky shape around the top of the pumpkin.

spiky shape

2 Ask an adult to carefully cut around the shape and lift off the top.

3 Cut off the top of the spikes on the bottom part of the pumpkin.

4 Scoop out the pulp and seeds inside the pumpkin with a spoon.

Tip: The more pulp you scoop out, the easier it is to carve the pumpkin.

5 Draw a pattern all over the bottom part of the pumpkin.

6 Ask an adult to cut out the shapes.

7 When it is dark, ask an adult to light a fat candle inside the pumpkin, so that the flame shines through the shapes.

Woven wonders

For thousands of years, people have created baskets from grasses and rushes, plants, and twigs. Some are woven or braided, others are coiled or twined.

☼ *This basket was made in Ecuador from sisal (cactus fibers), woven tightly together. Long ago, sisal bags were used to store dry food. Because the fibers swell and become waterproof when they are wet, people also used them to carry water.*

Look closer

- The brightly colored basket above has a zigzag pattern.
- The round basket on the right has a geometic pattern around the base and on the lid.

☼ *The design on this dried-grass sewing basket from India was made by dyeing the grass different colors.*

- The frame of the cow is made from coils of strong raffia grass and then covered with sikki grass.

- The cow has horns, nostrils, and even a tiny, red tongue.

✴ Women in India make coil baskets like this to take to their husbands' homes when they get married. The baskets are made of a golden-colored grass, called sikki.

✴ Baskets like this are known as "grandmother baskets" because they are only made by the older women of the Tonga people in Zimbabwe.

Look closer

- Wild grasses, reeds, and palm fronds were woven together to form the patterns on this basket.

- The dark parts were created from dye made from tree bark.

✴ This English wicker grocery basket was made from thin, bendy willow twigs.

A wicker basket being woven

19

Making a paper basket

Before you start, fold eight paper strips 3 x 9in (8 x 22cm) long and eight 3 x 5in (8 x 12cm) long, using magazine pages (see page 31).

1 Draw two circles around a cup on thin cardboard. Cut them out.

circles about 3in (8cm) across

2 Glue two of the 9in (22cm) long paper strips together to make a cross.

Make four crosses and glue them together to form a star.

3 Glue one card circle onto the top of the star and the other onto the bottom.

4 Fold up the strips. Hold them loosely together with a rubber band.

5 Weave a 5in (12cm) paper strip in and out of the upright strips. Glue the ends together.

6 Weave another strip above the first one, as shown. Glue the ends together.

7 Continue to weave until you have used all eight strips.

8 Leave two upright strips opposite each other for the handle. Cut off the rest, so they are about 1in (2cm) long. Glue them down.

9 Glue the two long strips together to make the handle.

Recycled designs

All these baskets and bowls were made from recycled paper, plastic, or wire.

This papier-mâché bowl was made in South Africa. It is decorated with pictures of fish cut out of sardine can labels. People sell these bowls to make money to help sick women and children.

Look closer

- Only the sardines have been cut out to create the fishy pattern.
- The fishes' heads all face in the same direction.
- The fish overlap each other.

- To create the design on this basket, the artist has grouped bright colors together.

- She rolled the pages tightly to make them thin and strong.

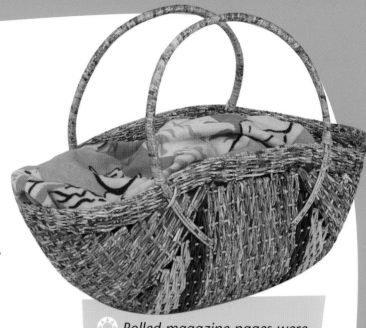

🌀 *Rolled magazine pages were woven together to make this basket from Vietnam.*

🌀 *This refuse basket was made in India from old plastic bags, paper, and straw.*

Look closer

- Each layer of this refuse basket is made from strips of plastic wrapped around coils of straw.

- The layers are held together by thin yellow plastic strips.

🌀 *These bowls are made from recycled telephone wire. Zulu nightwatchmen in South Africa started weaving like this, as something to do on their long night shifts.*

Look closer

- The swirling patterns on these bowls were created by weaving differently colored telephone wires together.

- The patterns are the same as those on traditional grass baskets.

telephone wires

A recycled wrapper bowl

You will need

- a plastic bowl ● plastic wrap
- white glue ● water
- newspaper ● magazines
- colorful candy wrappers
- white poster paint
- a paintbrush ● a glue pen

1 Tear newspaper into small pieces and put them into a pile. Tear pages from a colorful magazine into similar pieces. Keep these in a separate pile.

2 Cover the bowl with plastic wrap, making sure it overlaps the rim. Mix white glue with the same amount of water. Dip in the newspaper pieces and overlap them onto the bowl.

3 Once the bowl is covered with a layer of newspaper pieces, cover it with the magazine pieces. Alternate newspaper and magazine pieces until you have six layers altogether. Leave the papier-mâché bowl to dry.

Tip: The papier-mâché may take several days to dry.

4 When it is dry, separate the paper bowl from the plastic bowl. Trim the edges and paint the inside white. Let it dry.

5 Ask an adult to iron the candy wrappers flat under a cloth.

6 Glue candywrappers inside the bowl, overlapping one another, to make a colorful design. You may need to cut them to make them overlap neatly.

7 To make your bowl look glossy, cover it with a layer of the white glue mixture.

Lacquer boxes

These boxes are covered in layers and layers of lacquer. The lacquer makes them waterproof and strong, and helps to stop them from getting damaged.

Some lacquer is made from the sap of trees, some from the secretions of the lac insect.

☀ *Detailed pictures of fairytales, country life, landscapes, and even battles have been painted on the lids of miniature Russian boxes, like this one.*

Look closer

- The picture on the lid of the box above shows a girl carrying two milkchurns over the snow.
- In the distance, there are snow-covered houses and a church.

☀ *This black lacquer box, made in the 1800s, is decorated with paper flower cut-outs glued onto the surface and then covered with layers and layers of varnish. Each layer of varnish was finely sanded and polished. This is known as découpage.*

Look closer

- The flowers have been covered with so many layers of sanded varnish that they look as if they have been painted on the box.

These two wooden boxes from India are covered in lacquer made from the secretions of the lac insect. They hold red powder, called tilaka, which Hindu women put on the parting of their hair to show they are married.

Look closer

- Both boxes above are red. The lacquer was mixed with red oxide to give the box its color.

- The lacquer on the right-hand box has been carved to create a leafy design.

Look closer

- The mother-of-pearl flower decoration on the box below was cut and glued into the lacquer so that it is level with the surface. This is called inlay.

Made over 100 years ago, the black lacquer of this jewelry box has been decorated with pieces of shell cut from the pearl oyster, called mother-of-pearl, and rich gold paint.

A shiny star box

1 Paint the box black, inside and out. Let it dry.

You will need

- a cardboard box
- black paint and a paintbrush
- giftwrapping paper or old magazines
- scissors • a glue stick

Tip: You may need several layers of paint to cover the box completely.

2 Carefully cut out some colorful shapes or pictures from giftwrapping paper or magazines.

3 Lay the shapes in a design on the lid and sides of the box. Glue them down. Let the glue dry.

4 To make your box sturdy and shiny, brush on three layers of varnish. Allow each layer to dry before you brush on the next one.

Handy hints

Making paper pulp

1 Tear strips of newspaper into 1in (2cm) pieces, enough to fill about one-quarter of a bucket.

2 Ask an adult to cover them with hot water. When the water is cool, stir the mixture until it is soft and mushy.

3 Ask an adult to liquidize the mixture, a handful at a time, in a food processor until it is as smooth as possible.

4 Pour the mixture into a sieve. Press it with your fingers to squeeze out as much of the liquid as you can.

5 Put the pulp into a bowl and mix in a cup of white glue.

Tip: Keep any unused pulp in a sealed container in the fridge.

Paper strips for weaving

1 Fold over 1in (2cm) of the top edge of a magazine page. Fold the strip in half so that it is now ½in (1cm).

2 Glue along the paper, close to the edge of the folded paper strip.

3 Fold the strip over onto the glue. Cut off the strip.

Joining clay pieces together

To join two clay sausage coils together, first score both ends with a blunt knife. Wet both ends with water and push them together. Then smooth the joined pieces together.

Keep any unused clay in an airtight plastic bag. This will stop it from drying out.

Glossary

braid to interweave three or more long pieces of material, such as grass or twigs, together

calabash the fruit of a tree, often dried and used as a container for holding liquid

coil a length of clay, straw, etc., arranged in a circular or spiral shape

mold to shape into a form

sap the juice inside a plant or tree that helps it to grow and live

terra-cotta a type of reddish-brown baked clay. Terra-cotta means "baked earth"

twine strands of grass or plant fibers that have been twisted together

woven describes materials interlaced in two directions, widthways and lengthways

Index